2.00

Dream Catcher

Selected Poems by Lynn Kernan

Edited by Charlie Hertan

The Bunny and the Crocodile Press
Washington, DC

To my sister, Beth Fidoten, and her family; my "life support" crew, Robby Roiter, David Lovler, Jerry Rubin and his family, Sue ("Beast") Davis, and Jane Lynn.

Special thanks to Georgia Lee McElheny, Barb Feldman, Barry Whitebook, Ed Zahnizer, Ken Belliveau, Robert Krakauer, Grace and Cindy Cavalieri, Ethan Fischer, Patsy, Darlene, Jim, and all the Bookend Poets.

Contents

Part One: Snowscapes

Part Two: Elegy

Part Three: The Tarot Series: Major Arcana

Part Four: Dream Catcher

Part One

Snowscapes

Snowscapes

I.   Sleeper

How delicately
the snow subdues the land.
Only a solitary mocker seems to be aware
of its insidious draft
and tries to stare it down, then flees
with surrender's white wing flash.

How gently it invades
flinging back its flimsy spread,
inviting the bone-tired in.
"Here is purity," it whispers,
"here is peace."
I stare until snow blindness strikes,
close withered lids, lie down.

II.   Snow Angel

Slowly I slide arms up and down.
How marvelous! Wings on the ground,
glittering with crystals,
downed with intricate lace.
The angel child I always meant to be
will stare up at me
if I dare to stand,
new fallen, pure
from toe to crown,
Snow White, ready to rise at meltdown
on wings of shattering ice,
or hang around 'til March
growing dingier by the hour.

Evening at Shiloh

The peach orchard sighs,
sheds pink wings
that flutter in the breeze, alight,
blanket the weary ground.

Spring peepers shrill bright moon lust.
Whip-poor-wills keep vigil, chant.
Fresh dew stars the grass,
twinkles along the filaments
of a million cross threads
that dawn's grass spiders spread.
A shadow swoops,
guardian of the dead,
searching for live mice.

A puddle at orchard's edge
catches the sun's last breath,
absorbs crimsons,
blazes, a bloodbath.
The sun snuffs out its light.

Rainy Bus Ride

Turning my back to board the bus
I leave behind
a floating face,
dissolving words,
last spring's lilac buds.
The bus trembles,
leaves the curb:
the shape behind me blurs,
furs into a lily bloom
that rises from the gutter's mud.

The pavement shines,
we pass it by.
November's maples stain the grass
with clots of bright fall blood.
A glistening side road
snakes across the park,
glides to Manhattan's other side.
Always, always I leave love behind
and press forward toward its chest
with every breath.
The windshield weeps, the wipers
brush tears aside.

Fall Hollyhocks

They slouch along the fence line
at parade rest.
The summer silks of white and scarlet
which once divided them,
lie wrinkled on the ground.
With civies gone, they all look alike,
anonymous in baggy olive drab.
Their kelly swords have rusted, bent,
and shrunken to the size of shivs.

A stiff fall wind snaps them to attention
keeps them alert,
sensing winter's fray.
They wait in rows for marching orders
to come from higher up:
wait and stare across the lawn
like wizened Indian scouts.
Their seed pods tick like time bombs,
each hair triggered
to project its missiles on command:
to attack the green, green grass.

Survivor

I salvaged what I could:
my sanity,
a sprig of rosemary Ophelia dropped,
some old snapshots of lifelong friends:
whatever else I could when I went down.

I saw the ultimate calamity.
Saw the iceberg coming,
dry white death tearing the sky as it slid along.
Saw the pregnant bombers overhead,
the poison in the grass.
I wired my congressman,
shot flares,
wailed like a banshee.
No one cared,
so I dug underground.

Down in the cellar,
down with the rats, lost dreams and ruptured cans
I grew pale and thin,
digging in the coal bins for a bite to eat.
Grew myopic as a mole
while I dug in.
But, when it hit, I was prepared.

Years later I snuffled up for air.
Poked blindly at the polar cap that slipped
and ate the Western Hemisphere.
Fondled with albino hands
the treasures I still held:
my sanity, dried rosemary,
some limp snapshots with faded grins.

To My Cyclamen

(to Faith)

Go on then,
fly your flowers like fuchsia butterflies!
Perch on my bedroom sill
and flirt with winter's hungry sky,
make it suck with gray lips
at the window pane.
Laugh at the snow and sip green sap
up the straws of your crook-necked stems.
Pretend winter's a joke
played on the elderly.
Persuade me
God isn't really dead.

Bag Ladies

1st voice:
I once wore
gardenias in my hair
and received American Beauties
three dozen at a time.
Now I stand here in sneaks and withered socks,
in this wilted cotton with its bloom of stains,
a crimson bag clutched tight in a bouquet
against my chest
in case stray muggers strike.
My nose pressed flat against a nosegay of violets
behind a florist's glass.

2nd voice:
Sure, I was a hooker.
What else can you do when you're fourteen
and feel it's time to eat?
And I shot horse.
What would you do
if you screwed strangers every night,
watched their mouths crumple and collapse,
felt the drops from ruptured hearts
splatter on your chest?
When you felt your own nerve ends
curl up and short out?
It's not so bad, sleeping in the street.
Don't have to face a morning mirror
and the cops don't notice you
if no Johns are around.

3rd voice:
Once-upon-a-time
I'd stroller babies here.
Sit on this exact bench
in smart suede suits and a stenciled smile

chatting with other bright young wives,
while the children built castles in the sand
and, uptown, Bill forged on to bigger deals
and younger brides.
Now I come alone at night, and rise at dawn to find
a cortege of pigeons
crapping beneath my bed.

2nd voice:
Last night the street lamps gleamed like fairy lights
through the bottom of an empty Old Grandad
and somewhere in my head
a carousel went round and round
and the blue Danube waltzed.
This condemned floor was a cradle then,
soft as a feather bed.
Now the sunlight lasers me
and my brain's not clear enough to know
whether those rats are real.

1st voice:
Wonder what Mama would have said
to see me here with two kids under three?
When we were growing up
she worked for other folks
and still kept our place bone clean.
Swept the front yard every day
and raked symmetrical designs on it
like a Zen monastery.
I bet she would have managed somehow
to scrub and wax this floor
in the Port Authority.

3rd voice:
For some unknown reason,
after I tested positive
I decided to visit Mom again.
"I told you!" she said.

"God smites sin with ulcerated lips,
with brimstone bones and sores of flame
with withering of the flesh.
Unclean! Unclean! Don't come in here!"
She slammed the door.
Still, sometimes,
I think I hear a lullaby at night
when I spread out the sleeping bag she got me
to go to summer camp.

2nd voice:
The angel Gabriel hides
in that alley over there.
At night he burns and cries,
"Beware, beware, of the lady with flames for hair."
St. Veronica owns that little shop.
She closes the curtains in the windows every night
and paints the four-eyed face on them
and whistles while she works.
In the morning, she pulls the curtains back
and the face falls on the floor.
Jesus Christ sleeps in that garbage can.
He says, "Suffer the little children."
and when I was, I did.
There's always something going on here,
very interesting,
but it *was* warmer on the ward.

3rd voice:
"Save for your old age," they said.
We did.
Then Al got sick,
lay in Mt. Sinai three years
being breathed and fed.
Now he rests in Morningside Heights Cemetery
and I curl up for warmth against
a street vent winter nights.

Unexpected Snowstorm, 4:30 a.m.

For hours the clock's lain by my cheek.
It chatters like a nervous child
and with malicious little hands
keeps stretching minutes into hours.

Last night the moon lay with me,
filled the craters you had left with heavy, silver cream.
Tonight he stayed until I slept
then, like you, slipped away unseen.

My love, the sky is falling now
and smothering the ground
with comforters of leprous white:
treacheries of eiderdown.

Sink Hole

Here is the exact spot
where the earth caved in.
Trees staggered, tore their hair
and toppled. Air caught its breath
and plunged.
With one last skyward glance,
light closed its eyes and fell
Lay stunned on the frozen fingers
of shattered stalactites
then slid, drop by drop,
into the limestone catacomb:
became one with night.

That was long ago
the hole has healed,
its scars sleep under grass.
Honeysuckle pours its balm of greens
down the far edge.
From dead center
the tips of great oak trees
show above ground:
shelter the saplings they have sewn
which now rise from the depths.
In high wind or snow,
cattle graze within the sanctuary
of its upper lip.

The Gift

Yesterday you came with flowers;
with crimson roses,
still unopened,
clenched in both your fists.
All day long I watched them
falling in love with me
Watched them shyly bare,
one petal at a time,
their private parts,
their golden seeds
in a heedless rapture.
In the mindless dance
of a devotee.

Now they're exhausted. Nearly dead,
each marked for the final journey
by a map of wrinkles
and dark with bruises it does not understand.
Some have collapsed into small fists of pain.
Some chose the suicidal leap
and lie in broken curls
on the cold morning floor.
Not one survived the shock.
Such sudden opening.

And here you come again,
hands full of fresh cut victims,
eyes dim behind a life of bruises
you do not understand.
Closed like a bud,
a fighter's fist.
I do not want these flowers you bring
or their revelations.
I know the private face of death
and do not need the roses' blood,
the thorns' remembrance.

White Ptarmigan

Here, snow is friend.
I blend into it.
Burrow into its folds
as blizzards pass.
Hide in its heart of ice.
Emerge when the storm diminishes
to make tracks for the willow,
find frozen buds to eat.

Freeze when an Arctic fox
slinks into sight.
Crouch, mold myself into
another inconspicuous lump of white.
Fly when the tension grows too great.
Expose myself against a treacherous sky.
See, too late, the gyrfalcon,
the sun's glint on claws of ice.
Leave a single feather drifting
on the wind's eternal breath.

Part Two

Elegy

Manhattan Street Scene: November

The flower vendor,
a gnarled pine bent above
a passion of summer petals,
dreams of Vietnam.
He chafes worn hands above their blaze
until the thin white scars across the palms
soften, begin to glow.
His torn muffler twitches,
writhes in the hungry wind.
Overhead a canvas awning
cracks like red and green firecrackers
on a New Year's dragon,
like distant gunfire waking
the small hours of the night.

Nursing Home: Shadow of Death

(To Belle)

We live in the valley here.
Ancient Appalachians flow in blue swells around us
as they ground down to seabed again.
Our tenuous shadows come and go.
One of our remnant is wheeled out on a gurney
and does not return.
A sleeper forgets how to breathe one night.
In winter we cast pneumonia's bones
to see where they will fall.

As a survivor
I have learned to select my memories carefully:
only the bright blue ones that sparkle,
never irregular onyx blots.
I have learned to carefully choose
that which I observe:
the birds flying in on wings of light,
upright trees emerging
from thick morning mist.

Nursing Home: In the Lounge, 1:45 a.m.

A sideshow of insomniance,
the legless man,
the woman half-blown away,
Man Mountain Dean,
The Madwoman of Chaillot.

Man Mountain slouches in his chair
chin to chest.
He's trying to hide from his wife, Miss Lilly,
who, after sixty years of wedded bliss,
has perfected the art of domination.
In his inner ear a voice whines,
"Daddy, clog up to the desk
and find someone to come and fluff my pillow."
He raises his head and smiles,
thinking of the thousand and one techniques
to silence that voice forever.

The Madwoman has the aristocratic bearing
and the patrician bones that her part demands.
She nods her head graciously
and begins to converse with the television set.
She raises her arms gracefully:
"I have two arms," she says.
The TV set stares back, babbling to itself.

The legless man has nodded off.
He's appearing at City Center tonight
as the prince in Swan Lake.
He leaps into the air and holds his pose
then lands with such agility
the audience stands, applauds.
Now he's running down green astroturf,

football clenched to side.
He is running, running toward the goal,
but just before he gets there
he wakes up with a start.

The left-sided woman enters a mental maze,
the one about not smoking,
realizes she's paced this one a million times before,
reverses herself, returns to reality
and begins to write a poem.

Nursing Home: Today's Show

Ivan arrives at dawn
to report the news.
Eighty-five years of careful observation
have given him the keys to understanding
the weather's vagrancy.
He takes its temperature,
charts the breeze,
monitors the smoke signals
it puffs across the sky.
"It's going to rain, by cracky," Ivan says.
Next, a rundown
on the condition of failing patients,
the latest wheelchair collision,
Delia's current fantasy.
Then, a list of sightings:
two does, chipmunks, the gray groundhog,
a stray cat, a wild turkey.

Later, in the corridor,
I see Ivan standing at the east end window,
weight propped on the windowsill,
wheelchair left behind.
As its face clears the mountain before him
Ivan salutes the sun.

Pondering Forbidden Fruit

Still, after this bony rosary of years,
that sudden hiss in the heart, "Take me.
Devour me. I am succulence incarnate,
the cessation of desire."
Key turned, old gears grind and mesh.
Like a rusty automaton I lurch forward,
licking cracked lips;
saliva glistens, drops.

When this withered flesh has been shucked, cast aside,
I wonder if my body of light
after eons beneath the Boddhi tree
will hear the ultraviolet aura of some fig
murmuring, "Taste me."

Peonies

The peonies are out,
pink comforts of my early years
that reappeared with such exact
regularity:
waxed green globes that mushroom,
show rosy seams
and split,
shake out plumes of pink
delicate as silk,
translucent flamingo wings
that darken, wilt,
melt and shed wet petals,
oriental tears.

Guernica

The horse with a blade for a tongue
still pierces my dreams.
And the woman, immobile as a wailing wall,
bolts welded to iron nipples,
the milk of kindness shut off at its source,
limp fingers swollen, splayed,
inept to stroke a child, to cradle grief.
And the baby oozing from her arms will no longer scream
for food or love or breath,
so young for such a sleep.
The city has floundered, capsized.
Flames sprout like weeds from uprooted sidewalks.
Trees tangle with truncated stairs.
All exits lead nowhere.
Above it all, a bare light bulb
glows on its slender wire,
brilliant, burning, intact,
star of the east to guide
through the enveloping night.

Incensed

If you touch me,
I will unfold great petals
that shake out clouds of incense
to saturate the sky,
engulf the moon with ecstasy,
cause the stars to thrill:
and this commercial message comes
from Hexacholorasphyll.

To tell the truth, I smell like an animal,
never floral and rarely odor free:
do not stuff my womb with cloves
or carry dried rose in my mouth
like an empty jar.
If you want musk, go rent an ox.
Try Lysol for that sanitary void.

CBS Newscast 2-16-99

1.   The Child

Barely twelve, she is alone
when the bag ruptures.
Water cascades down her legs,
runs off in rivulets
mapping the kitchen floor.
She understands that it is too late
to evaporate,
lie like a shadow beneath the bed,
storm the Pearly Gates.
She delivers herself.

Newborn she lies
in a grocery bag.
It breathes about her,
rises and falls, spilling pooled black shadows
from stiff plastic folds.
They seep into the gummy floor
of the garbage bin.
She screams, the bag bursts,
She is heard.
Already born again, she delivers herself.

2.   The Father

When he raped her,
he was twenty-nine.
Eighteen when he created her,
another human being.
One tries to understand.

Lust dug spurs in.
Fury unsheathed its claws.
There was no annunciation.

Conception occurred in a flash,
a fumbling, the smell of burning flesh
in the alley of shadows
or in the feral blackness of Bloods' den
where the others face remains a mystery,
or at home curled in the arms
of the mother-to-be
while moonlight flowed across the bed.
Time twists and turns,
pierces the heart,
corkscrews through the brain.
He took his daughter on the kitchen floor and fled.
Only a pool of first blood
and the footprints of the fugitive remained.

3.   The Mother

The first time she wailed,
like a siren sighting a bomb,
at seven understanding only
that the monstrous had occurred.
Later her normal flow began,
beyond blessing or curse
it seemed a stream of death in life.
Awesome her scrawny body
could remember through perdition
the secret of the sacred mysteries.
Could it still bear weight?

The moon is treacherous,
lulling us with its relentless cycle
until the magical dwindles to commonplace.
She forgot things Eleusinian,
went salvaging for love through garbage bins,
through the Bloods' territory of traps.
She ran howling with the pack.

Bodies came and went.
Children peeked out, like bewildered flowers,
from between her crimson thighs.
The moon was full the night her first
grandchild was bagged and reappeared.
She had slipped on her necklace of polished bones,
pinned a gardenia in her hair,
and followed the gilded sidewalk once again,
to the proper corner
to peddle a pound of flesh.

Unmarked Confederate Graves Near Shepherdstown, West Virginia

Here elms shade unrecorded graves.
All that remains of unsung heroes
rests beneath cows' hooves, cropped grass.
Chalky fingers twine in tap roots now
having released the old days,
gray shadows,
daguerrotypes of the past.

Limestone outcroppings stand as monuments,
as sentinels,
as honor guard.
Their austere, weathered faces are lichen bearded,
fossil pocked.
Patiently they listen
for Armageddon's reveille;
stare uphill at a crumbling barn
haunted by mourning doves.

Conversation

A friend and I speak of scars.
Hers are decorative,
velvety fire petals
on a battlefield of snow.
Mine are strictly practical,
a stagger of cross stitches done
in the hum-drum greens of surgery.
We both have learned that scars
sing with silent tongues,
glow when the moon is full,
do not vanish overnight.
We both have come to understand
the scalpel as necessity
to the cutting free.

Blue Glass Bowl

It slipped and fell:
broke into a pool of pieces,
a pond of blue that widened
across the kitchen floor.

I waded in,
swept up the shattered waves
and buried them beneath the coffee grounds.

And if the sky fell
it would be the same.
There I'd be, on hands and knees,
wondering how I'd dropped the thing.
Or flashing an obsequious smile
while sneaking dustpanfuls of blue
outside to the garbage can.

Mourning Dove

You don't mourn. Believe me
I know grief and it's no dove.
No smoky voice
curling through spring dawns,
drifting with the wildflower mists that rise
to bless the newborn sun.
No phantom silhouette, gray at high noon,
hidden among the silence of the pines,
or haunting, with a final breath,
the purple shadows of the evening sky.
Grief calls no mate. Says no prayers.
Knows no lullaby.
It does not vanish even when I stare.

Grief stays and stays
and alters not one line.
Black etching, by sulfuric hands,
hard edged on a winter sky
each feather cruel,
each barb claw red with death.
Its beak cracks no bone. It never sleeps.
It has no voice at all.

Warning to a Peach Orchard (In a Very Warm December)

It is too soon to redden:
to bud: blush top to tap root and stretch out
pink slips toward the sun,
grab for it like a hungry lover.
This spring is false, a cheat:
a fake of holy blue heisted from the sky
of some medieval masterpiece:
some illumination
of haloed saints, horned dragons,
and a virgin, early wise,
(hands cupped about the bud she bears)
who's looking fixedly at that sky
with a mysterious smile.

Too soon! This sun will fade,
dwindle to a pale December dot and disappear.
And you will be left with gravid arms extended,
waiting to be brought to fruit by a sky gone gray:
left to splatter ruby buds
on winter's marble head:
left to hold his leafless hands
and stroke his grizzled cheeks
with your thin red shoots that curve
up, like a secret smile.

Part Three

Tarot Poems: The Major Arcana

#0 - The Fool's Tale

I shot the swan in ignorance.
Sequestered since birth,
I was unable to observe that Death is real.
White wings of grace fluttered, failed.
All that loveliness
fell from the sky.
A murky red stain blossomed
around the feathered shaft,
I plucked it out;
sucked at the breast,
white drifts of down, warm sticky wine.
It lay quite still,
only a few wing feathers
danced in the soft spring wind.

I wept and pierced myself,
and that was, really, the beginning of the tale;
start of a quest that's led now
through the Forest of Darkness,
across the River Red,
knowing every footfall may crush some burnished beetle,
some incandescent flower:
forced to hunt for the elixir
that will end this bleeding;
to search for forgiveness
from the Holy Grail.

#6 - The Lovers

Adam and Eve between two yews,
in the garden, the portal of death.
Already they know they must wear flesh,
cover themselves as they stand apart.
Above Eve, a unicorn,
purity wearing a satyr's horn.
Above Adam, a crimson rose
trapped on a staff of thorns.

They hold a golden chalice toward heaven,
a challenge, a Grail,
a loving cup.
The Sky God thrusts his flaming spear,
the wine ignites, burns out.

And so the lovers must always stand
between the trees of time,
supplicating the spirit
while rooted to the ground,
condemned to seek for wholeness
in the circle of magic
formed by their embrace.
Yin and Yang in Tantric flames;
in perpetual dance.

#9 - The Hermit on Night Mountain

Up, forever up,
groping through these folds of mist,
thick swirls that swallow the waning moon,
snuff Orion out.
Trees cluster in,
whisper to the shades that sigh beneath them
claw with gnarled roots at my staff.
My lantern casts gold coins
along the path.

Fireflies mass above damp grass,
each signaling for a mate.
Tree frogs pipe desire.
I envy them, but pole on up the mountain,
place of unknown wings
that brush by in the darkness
place of dry stones beneath tired feet.

#11 - Justice

Peacock feathers tremble
like exotic petals
upon a tree of life.
Their eyes are unclear,
they penetrate.
I'm frightened by their stare.
Before them hangs a jeweler's scale,
one pan silver,
one of gold,
an alchemist's measure.
A soul is being balanced here.

Both pans are suspended
on elaborate chains
hooked to a slender, silver shaft:
we sway in them.
Above us, from the center of the shaft
winks a giant pearl,
tear of some judicial god
who may wear a blindfold now
but once could see,
could weep.

#12 - The Hanged Man: (Headdown on Ygdrasil)

For so long have I hung
that my hair is rooted to the ground,
my toenails have pierced this oak.
The North Wind has stripped me of desire.
The South Wind burned away my need
to bend things to my will,
Now I sway freely in the breeze
ripening like fruit.

I have released my ravens, Thought and Memory,
and watched them dwindle to inkspots
in a sky of sunset reds.
Daily I contemplate the taproot itself.
Beneath it lies the holy well,
rune guard, fount of knowledge,
keeper of the keys.
It will yield its secrets only to the one
whose wisdom has been earned through statis;
through prolonged meditation while suspended mid-air,
trapped between sky and ground.

#13 - Death

A river.
Charon drifts by in his barge
conveying dust from here to there.
The flow in which we float
is one from source to mouth;
forever singing as it goes,
forever seeking rest.
I watch the reeds
swaying above me on the bank.
An arm of skinny bones
raises a scythe and severs them.
They float beside me for a while,
grow sodden, disappear.

On the bank saunters a peacock.
An iridescent feather loosens,
settles to the ground.
Already another is growing in.
His tail shimmers, a long flow in his wake,
ripples like a stream.
He is all eyes.
They watch me disappear.

#14 - Alchemy: (Temperance)

"...alchemy...has but one aim: to extract the quintessence of things; to prepare arcana, tinctures, elixirs capable of returning man to the health he has lost."   -- Paracelsus

I am hermaphrodite,
the point of crystallization that lies
beyond duality.
In me the base and pure combine,
sulfur unites with mercury.
I am the white stone and the red,
the solar and the lunar tree.
Cremated in the egg,
I hatch in purity.

I entered the crucible as pitch;
at my conjunction clarified,
flamed into a peacock's tail.
Knowledge of the fire turned me to snow,
purified beyond pain's reach.
Transmuted, I turn to gold.
Powder me fine
and make a tincture with but a single pinch.
It will transform fragility
into courage for the quest;
alleviate your growing pains,
the throb of loneliness.

#16 - The Tower

This, then, is the modern Tower of Babel,
construct of reinforced concrete,
of arrogance and steel;
skyscraper spired for its assault on heaven.
There is darkness here...
ruin...
devastation.
Can this card be reversed?

From the tower fly flags of many lands.
I throw the window open,
look down on them,
multi-colored streamers flowing in a razor wind;
forked tongues flickering above abandoned concrete canyons
where ticker tape parades once lived.
There is darkness here.

Outside the door
snow blows down the empty corridor.
Wild dogs have made their dens
behind the mainframe.
The Board Room has been commandeered
by cockroaches and mice.
Somewhere, in an upper room,
the remnant is praying now
for enlightenment.
Can this card be reversed?

#17 - The Sun in Spring

Yearly, I return to dance
in a saffron robe,
with finger cymbals flashing in my hands.
Lord of the Sufis, King of the Crimson Rose.
Below me in the garden,
a breeze begins.
My devotees shiver,
throw back their heads and dance.

I touch a bud;
slowly it turns and nuzzles my glow.
Its closed heart stirs;
the outer petals unfurl, tremble in the wind.
I slip deeper into the folds
until the rose
flames into a full blown beauty.
Such a rapture of silks!
Such incense smoldering from the sacred heart,
open to me now, all thoughts of winter gone
all memories of hibernation
beneath pack ice and snow.

#18 - The Moon

The night sea melts my silver.
Dissolves it into a flash of ripples,
a flow of scales, a fish.
Enamored, the sea would mold me
into one of its own.
How it trails after me,
yearns toward me when I disappear.

Goddess of its mysteries,
I alone speak to the bubbling vents
that talk in tongues;
wrap myself in garlands of sea anemone,
lethal iridescent flowers;
divide where barnacled antiquities
hide in drifts of coral,
in caves of sand;
peer into primordial depths
where prehistoric monsters glide.

The waves sigh my litany.
Oysters, inside their iridescent shells,
shape, even as they sleep,
my sacred image
which they, in dreams, embrace.

#19 - The Star

I am waiting to be born.
Behind my veil,
this luminous birth caul,
I crystallize,
spin a unique shape.
I have said goodbye
to my seven sisters.
We wept and parted.
They watch me now, prepare to celebrate
my emergence into light.

There is a new earth
to be created, a new self.
It will be beautiful,
transparent water and immaculate stone
untouched by any hand.
I will take a ritual bath
in the pool of forgetfulness,
then its waters will teem with life.

When I rise, drops will stream from me,
splatter on the stones,
create a random pattern from which
a universe could come.
But now I wait, exhausted,
gather strength to blaze,
to rise again in the East.

Part Four

Dream Catcher

Last Fishing Trip

All day long we floated on
The tensile silence of the lake:
you catching bream
and tossing them back again;
tangling tackle in tackle,
boat in line,
yourself in old strings from the past:
while I watched the sun
shatter on the waves;
memorized, for future use,
the silence of the pines;
froze to point when a blue heron
settled in the shallows and,
elegantly, began to stalk for bass.

As the sun set, we floated back to shore,
unlocked stiff limbs,
lurched up the bank:
you limp as the sinker lines
leaking from the tackle box,
me dull as the drying skin
of a dead rainbow trout.
As we turned toward the woods to leave
an osprey soared out of their inks
into the sun's blood light:
shrieked once and plunged,
flaming like a meteor,
from the darkening sky
into the still black lake.

Form Without Color

At night
my amaryllis cannot shout its scarlets.
It is lovely still,
slender and elegant in black.
Before going color blind, I would have longed
to warm my eyes against such reds.
Now I am content to sit and watch
its delicate lily face
praying in moonlight.

The Persistence of Questions

If I'd been there
would I have dared to even think, "No More!"?
To refuse to snitch to S.S. men
in their Darth Vader helmets,
flashing their switchblade smiles?

Would I have dared to cloister nuns beneath my bed,
roast Krupp in his own oven,
even show a nappy head?

Dared salute Mother Russia,
defend the Eiffel Tower,
stretch out a hand to feel the burns
of David's falling stars?

Would I have smuggled Poland to the Alps?

Or would I have sat,
smug as a Hummel figurine
on the front verandah
to sip Courvoisier
and smoke black market cigarettes,
smugly hoarded heavy cream
while pedaling watered milk?
Would I have sold my soul
for thirty silver pieces?
Waxed exceeding fat?

Aging

Without specs, it's hard to tell
which are dried leaves settling
after their final ecstatic twirl
with the North Wind,
and which are sparrows,
fence-rail sitters,
fluttering to earth seeking sustenance.
Ears help. The sparrows bicker among themselves.
The dead leaves contentedly
whisper, "Bismillah."

Reverberation

My wind chime
is singing in the pine.
It pretends its Japanese,
tries to sound like a samisen and fails.
Graceful as a geisha, it teases any breeze,
tinkles its intimate secrets
to stray starlings, bedraggled cats.
On windless days it remains entirely mute
causing the sunshine to dwindle just a bit.

Tree Magic/Druid's Choice

One friend slept beneath the thorned crowns
of a dogwood tree,
imbibed a quart of white lightning
and was struck
by enlightenment.

Another chose the oak,
dreamed of Gwydion, Prince of Air,
and awoke to find herself a shape shifter
with mistletoe, like small moons,
shining in her hair.

My Father, ancient Kabbalist,
chose the Tree of Life,
then spent the traditional four score years
and seven
determinedly hoisting himself higher, higher,
until he came to Kether and vanished,
shot straight up through the crown.

Being oversensitive,
I chose that arbiter of grace, the weeping willow,
and hang around as near the top as possible,
so transfixed by its beauty that
I'm confident of that white flash.

July Fourth

Above us bloom giant cockscombs,
chartreuse chrysanthemums,
dry dandelion heads.
They open with a heavy metal glare.
Fire petals blaze, wilt quickly, shed,
fall like stars about us.
Pollen of ash,
gunpowder scents,
drift in the hazy air.
Between these martial detonations
fireflies flash silent passion,
the full moon rises red.

Day in the Life of the Poet Laureate

(to GLM)

Salutes the sun.
Lights cigarette.
Mislays glasses.
Talks to cats.
Makes calls, dresses, hustles out.
Buys bird food, five hundred pounds.
Saves Shepherdstown.
Returns at sunset,
stares out the window at the flowers.
Retires.
Rises at 3:00 a.m. to write by moonlight,
laurel leaves shining in her hair.

Dream Catcher

My dream catcher's thick with dust,
fly husks. Its cobweb
cannot seine silver from the dreams
of one who never sleeps.
Black silk shadows dangle
from its lower edge,
flutter before the moon's breath
like tattered silhouettes.

Spider Woman, the soul catcher,
crouches to the left of center.
She's famished now,
a scarecrow of her former self:
set to pounce on any random vision,
any illusion of nourishment
that tangles in her trap:
threatening, unfed, to net my shadow,
thread it to flaunt its stains and tattered edges
beside the others dangling there.

Grey fears flutter by,
moths of the mind that fly at 4:00 a.m.
when one cannot sleep;
shades of the hopelessness that lures
one to wing instinctively
toward Spider Woman's web.

To escape, I must dare again
The midnight tunnel of the vision quest
brave the ritual piercing,
confront the shades that lay hearts bare.
I take the spider as my totem:
Become my own Eucharist
and feed myself unto myself.

Iranian Minefield Walkers

I, too, who already pace this minefield
heart in hand,
neck pious in prayer,
would know I walked for God:
know this blind man's bluff through
the territory of traps
was for a sacred cause.

Then I could glide
with the innate balance,
the delicate restraint
of all tightrope walkers:
eyes dead ahead on Paradise,
ear on the cricket's chirrup that counts
the seconds to burying ground.
Then I could walk the slack wire
of Fate's apron strings
while juggling my life in epileptic hands.
Then I could levitate,
strike lightning,
find the holy field on which
I, too, with impunity,
could simply disappear.

Mystery Poem: Christmas 1983

Like Christ himself, the stars are born
beyond a shimmering veil
of their own cosmic dust;
are ordinary miracles
swaddled to mystify the Judas heart,
the evil eye,
the whittler intellect
that cuts things down to size.

New born they rise to glory
and startle the dead of night;
start vision quests among the wise
who, following their hearts,
begin the endless trek to find
just where new starlight struck our earth,
just where the new sun lies.

Sobriety is a State of Grace

The wolf pack held at bay,
the dove descends, daily,
clutching its olive branch.
Flood waters ebb,
mountains bare battered heads,
trees sun-dry their hair.

Slowly the ark
settles and gives birth.
Its load of life disembarks,
troops off to the wedding dance.
God's rainbow rises in the East.
Spring stalks the land.
Grape vines blossom,
put on leaves;
Judas trees bleed flowers.

Zen Manual

If you sit still enough:
you can see the earth spin;
each separate color a hummingbird
S.O.S.'s in frantic flight;
the Navajo patterns lightning scrawls
racing down to strike.

If you sit long enough you can:
learn how a willow cutting becomes
a tree of life;
watch the Mississippi River
eat out its own mouth;
observe how a priceless pearl is spun
around a grain of grit.

If you sit quietly enough
you can hear night crawlers groan
as they bulldoze earth;
the hiss of falling stars, God's breath;
the rustle of rust blooms opening
to clog the cannon's mouth.

Biography

Born in 1934, Lynn Kernan grew up in rural Virginia, West Virginia, and Kentucky, the daughter of Presbyterian minister Charles W. Kernan, and Elizabeth "Tibby" Kernan, a religious educator. After studying drama at Mary Baldwin College in Virginia, she met and married Don Hertan, the son of first generation Jewish immigrant parents, to the consternation of both sets of parents. The marriage fell apart in 1969 after 10 years and two children, and Lynn obtained a Fine Arts degree and taught art in an inner city school in New Jersey until suffering from debilitating back injuries. Struggling with pain and depression for many years, she coped by writing poetry and creating an exquisite portfolio of visual art in a variety of media, including oils, watercolor, weaving, pottery, and collage.

A great lover of nature and aesthetics, Lynn was well versed in classic literature, poetry, spiritual traditions, film, and art.

Returning to West Virginia in the late 1970s, she became a beloved member of the Bookends Poetry Group in Shepherdstown, WV, and one of the most respected West Virginia poets. At age 40, Kernan made a commitment to write for two hours a day, which she kept for the next 28 years. In 2001, suffering from terminal illness, Lynn moved to a nursing home in Massachusetts, where she continued to compose and dictate poetry from memory, being too frail to read or write. She died in Leeds, MA, in 2002, a day before her 68th birthday.

An annual memorial poetry gathering is held near Shepherdstown, WV, at the end of April, to celebrate her legacy. A modest artist, Lynn put relatively little emphasis on disseminating her work, once saying in an interview, "I figure my poems will reach the people who need them." Though her poems have appeared in many journals, including *Pivot*, *Bohemian Bridge*, *Potomac Review*, and the West Virginia Anthology *Wild Sweet Notes*, this is the first full book of her poetry.

Notes

The "Tarot Poems" were inspired by meditations on the richly illustrated Tarot deck of Hermann Haindl. Lynn became a devoted Tarot reader later in life and was widely sought by her community for spiritual readings.

Despite its eerie resonance, Tarot Poem #16, "The Tower," was written long before the tragedies of 9/11/01.

"Day in the Life of the Poet Laureate" is dedicated to distinguished West Virginia poet Georgia Lee McElheny.

The "Nursing Home" poems were composed and dictated from memory to G. L. McElheny and Ken Belliveau.